THE TWELVE POUND CIGARETTE

Poems by Ann Darr

The
Twelve
Pound
Cigarette

SCOP Publications, Inc.
College Park, MD

The Twelve Pound Cigarette
Cover Design: Donal McLaughlin
Photo: Robert Russell
Author Photo: Irv Broughton
Typography: Gabriele Glang

ISBN 0-930526-14-7
LC #90-052932

Grateful acknowledgment is made to the following publications:
Antietam Review: "The Spelling Lesson"
The Devil's Millhopper: "That Corner on the Fansler Road,"
"Hannibal, MO"
5 A.M.: "The Twelve Pound Cigarette"
The New Virginia Quarterly: "The Feminist Mistake"
Nimrod: "Winter Passage Out of Charlotte Amalie"
Ploughshares: "At Lunch You Talked About a Shoeshine in Chicago," "She
of the Flawed Character"
Poet Lore: "Logbook Turned to Feathers"
Poetry Now: "At Sixteen"
KINESIS, Ltd., *Radishes and Flowers:* "Wallace in Lilliput"
Radcliffe Quarterly: "Grandmother's Organ"
Farber & Farber, *Deep Down:* "At Sixteen"
SCOP Publications, Inc., *Free State:* "That Corner on the Fansler Road"
SCOP Publications, Inc., *Rye Bread:* "Drake Estate," "First the O"
SCOP Publications, Inc., *Second Rising:* "Waiting"

The author wishes to express her gratitude to the artists' colonies of
Yaddo and MacDowell for residencies during which some of these
poems were written. This book was made possible in part by the con-
tributions from: Quad Construction Corporation, Leonard Kapiloff
Foundation, Grady Management, Inc., and The Seldeen Organization.

SCOP FIFTEEN in a series
Printed in the United States of America
SCOP Publications, Inc.
Box 376, College Park, Maryland 20740

CONTENTS

In memory of my mother
Lessie Rebecca Hooper Russell
born 1888 in Guthrie County, Iowa
died 1923 on the Fansler Road

STORM WARNING

Here it comes again, my raw-
boned poetry, with arms akimbo
and legs knock-kneed. And though
in a sudden small swift sharp squall
Aphrodite lies with Amelia
on my floor, looking like the same
woman, is indeed the same woman,
with the square jaw-bone,
the liquid mouth, the curls across
the temple, I will leave out
all reference to the gods, male
and female and rely on whatever
myth hovers above the work, where
I too hover, raw bones and all.

THAT CORNER ON THE FANSLER ROAD

Dancing was not Methodist, nor
the Methodists for dancing. Even
the Graduation Banquet had speeches,
songs, no dance. So we sneaked off
to the wildest spot in the woods,
the old Fansler Dance Hall, forbidden
as any place ever was. For good reason.
Drinking and fist fights and bottle
throwing and burning, an easy place
to lose an eye or a leg or virginity
by violence. Our innocence protected
us a little. When the river rose
and wiped out the settlement —
the chicken farmers and those with
turkeys, the splintered old dance
floor — the Methodists knew it was
a heavenly stroke for virtue.

But the corner of the Fansler road
was graveled into place and even
the river's flooding waters couldn't
wash away the menace of that corner
where the old Hudson with all of us
in it — Uncle B, Aunt M, Cousin J,
Mama and me — couldn't at that speed,
didn't make the turn and we ploughed
ground, over and over into the ditch,
rolling as if in time to some apple-
jack rhythm orchestrated by Uncle B
who dried out later, too late for Mama
who in that ancient Hudson did a fancy
dance through glass.

                    And I dance,
I drink and dance on the deck of
the *m.t.s. Orpheus*, throw my bottle
overboard into the Aegean, and watch it
drown in the wake.

AT SIXTEEN

We come now to the space which is boy-shaped.
It has always been there, filled or unfilled.
Come ride with me on my motor-cycle, we'll do
the whole mile-square by moonlight and we rode,
I clinging to that boy shape with all the girl
shape I was, and the moon made shadows of us
on the corn rows, and we scared ourselves on
the corners, and laughed as loud as we dared
and swung on home before the night could get us.
In the wane of that same moon, he raced the mile alone
and struck an old car parked without its lights
and the night got him, and the moon had to shine
a great many nights before I was sure it wouldn't
get me too. We had been little kids together,
sitting flat out in my sandbox, making pies.
We practiced kissing in the alley behind his house
and mine. I can still hear the little lights
in his voice that made my nipples stand out straight.

TEMPERATURE INVERSION

I shopped for a week to find
the right excuse to wear to come
to your bedside and touch your hand,
something in my best color, blue,
but everything I carried home
was red, insulting, raw. I returned
them all for credit.
What big polka dots, you said,
when I finally turned up
in my checkered best.

> The past turns colors
> according to the wind.
> Ignorance distorts
> the images. The road
> is cut through virgin land.
> Meadow-larks are
> singing everywhere.
> I can tell by your eyes
> you cannot hear them.

And so I have arrived
on this green prairie where names
are more familiar than those of
my current friends. How could we
have thought this gentle incline
could have been named "hill"?

I see again pink pleated elegance of small
lamp shades over filigreed silver,
pink pleated skirts of elegant girls
I envied, yearned to be like. But I was
busy sewing myself into a bag, stitching
up a sack in which to deliver my soul
to the word junkies.

Your eyes surprise me.
In them I recognize
the temperature inversion:
I forgive you. I had thought
I would ask you to
forgive me.

HANNIBAL, MO

This morning I wandered Cardiff
Hill with its twenty-foot statues of
Tom and Huckleberry, walked
through the tiny house the Clemens
called home. "Everyone was poor," he wrote
"but they didn't know it." Into focus
came the trips I went on from Bagley
to Missouri in the Roaring Twenties,
and after, in the Great Depression,
when we were poor and did know it.
Black cotton stockings, outing flannel
underwear, tied-together belts to pull
on and off the light bulb hanging
from the ceiling, so the dark couldn't
get us. The outhouse, the windmill,
the corn huskers, threshing dinners,
piles of steaming food in the middle
of the hot hot day, men dripping sweat
washing at the tub on the wooden bench
by the tree, the roller towel
by the back door.

                    And hear again
the tick/tick/tick/ of the grasshoppers
in the corn, ticking as they ate from
leaf to leaf, stripping the corn crop,
the strickening sound of their appetite.
Nothing to stop them. Nothing.
My papa, helpless man, chewing
on his wrist in the twilight, rocking
on the porch in his twilight,
rocking rocking to the tick/
tick/tick of the grasshoppers
wiping out the crop.

THIS IS NO DEPRESSION, SHE SAID

Found Poem, Interview

This is no depression.
I went through one,
so I know. The summer
of 1930 was dry. We
watered our limas, kept
them going when
no one else had anything.
Two neighbors,
my mother and I
sat up all night
and shelled
a hundred and five
quarts. We took them
into town, to Jake Hyman
who had a store.
I drove the machine up.
He offered us 25 cents
a quart. "The only way,"
I said to Jake, "is to
take them, every blamed one.
Or I'll tramp the streets
and sell them door to door."
He said, "Oh lady,
that's a helluva lot
of beans." I said,
"I found that out
last night."

My parents had a cleaning shop
at the time. My mother
missed one of her customers
and went by to see if she
was all right.
The lady began to cry.
She had killed their
little dog and was cooking
it on the stove. Well,
there was not much we could do,
so we didn't think about it
a great deal. We sat there
and lived.
That was the Depression.

WAITING

I am through with magic.
This time I will not run the movies
through my head, the bloody plots,
flaming ships, gunshot wounds, boil-
ing oil, burial alive, icicles
through the chest, all to ward off evil.
I can finally let the magic go. Now I know
I am not that powerful.

The hours drag by. The ironing board
squeaks as I bear down
on the striped sleeve of this shirt,
back and forth, back and forth,
flip the shirt to engage the yoke,
steam sizzles out of the iron,
stripes gleam under pressure,
the hours drag, the phone
does not ring.

Shirt after shirt hangs like
a headless chorus. The sheets
stack in smoothed piles on the shelves.
The phone does not ring. What
has gone wrong at the hospital?
No one dies in childbirth anymore.

I am struck with error. Of course
I am that powerful. I should have
muttered all the magic rhymes I know,
carried out the incantations all witches
learn. I should have buried the bloody cloths,
run three rings around the whiskey bush,
prayed. Now I begin the concentration
meant to save her life. All the strength
I felt when she was born floods through me
floods through to her. I throw my reason
on the floor and glory in the power. The phone
rings. She is safely delivered of a son.

I pick up my reason from where I had thrown it,
drape it around my shoulders, knowing
I will never tell anyone.

GRANDMOTHER'S ORGAN

Today I have uncrated the old organ,
making it groan into the atmosphere
above the old Blue Ridge where it
came from. Its name is Edna. It
says so on the brass plaque. She
is dressed in the same red velvet
curtains (framing her diamond face)
tied back with blue faille ribbon,
that she started out with, was it
a hundred years ago? The dust from
the splintering of packaging slats
does not settle all of a piece, it
seems to hover over figures in
the air which stand for a moment
before they disintegrate into wood
shavings and old songs. There is
one carcass caught in the works
of the bellows. It may be
an Iowa mouse — or a Virginia
mouse, it is too far gone to tell
whether it pinioned itself on
an old barbed chord, or froze
to death in the barn where
these crates have been stored
all these years, waiting for
me to get out my hammer and
my desire. I can open these
boxes now without falling
into disrepair. The faces
that come through the old
diamond-shaped mirror can no
longer stare me down, make me
wince with guilt, wilt with
sorrow. I no longer feel
other quivering fingers on these

keys as I play. My wrinkled hands
fit into them like gloves. I may have
lived through enough of bends
in the bone, the grazing of the eyes,
the peeled skin, to not have to
do it anymore. I rock on the old
carpeted pedals, Edna and I groan
together. I pull out all the stops
and begin to sing.

THE TWELVE POUND CIGARETTE

I am standing under the pear tree
watching the glow in my hand, a red star
I can manipulate, swing back and forth
like my own meteor swirling through sky,
how far are the true stars from my star,
are they as dangerous as mine?
My watch says one-thirty-three, luminous
numerals catching the gleam from the arc
light lighting the barnyard. What am I
doing out here in the mostly dark yard
in the middle of the night, making my own

clouds, making my own star, my own meteor,
I am out here playing with fire, foolish
woman that I am. I am here because
my daughter who lives on this farm, in this
farmhouse has set down rules. She is
ruler of this household when her husband
is away, and sometimes when he isn't and she

has birthed two children on this Virginia
farmland and does not allow anyone to smoke
in her house. She has also birthed a number
of lambs and the night she lost one when
she was carrying her own overdue son, she
stood and cried till the tears ran down
and hit the hard earth at her feet
and the meadow echoed with her shriek.
She was alone with the ailing ewe and death
stood by the barnyard light-pole smoking
his cigarette.

LOGBOOK TURNED TO FEATHERS

In the dream my logbook turned to feathers
and I flew

close formation with a band of angels
flying home.

We did wingovers under bridges on the Nile
and pylon eights around the Taj Mahal.

Wingtip to wingtip we headed for the sun
with visibility

unlimited of planets yet unknown.
In a blaze

that seared my eyes to blisters
they were gone

through gates I couldn't follow
and I fell

through haze, through clouds, through time.
I could not tell

whether the gates were heaven or
were hell,

but I was caught in Leonardo's gaze
and Goddard's skull was tolling like a bell.

THE SPELLING LESSON

You know I really believed that stuff,
that if your initials spelled something,
you'd be rich? So starting out with
an L and an A and an R, I threw all
those sheep's eyes (that's what we called
the hungry look) at that young Klinger
boy. I don't know how he knew all
he knew. Surely his older brothers
couldn't have taught him all. But
I was glad he was part of my growing
up. For I truly loved him, and he me,
there for several days that spring
and summer. And we were warm and tender
and trembled when we saw each other coming.
And we would walk hand in hand around the little dark
town and anticipate. As for simple love,
there is none better.
                    Years later
in a mess hall in Las Vegas,
catching a bite before our towing
target run, I said to my co-pilot,
"There is the back of a neck I recognize."
She called me crazy, said she didn't care
to fly with me again. We made a bet.
And when he walked out of that mess hall,
he was my young man beginning with K.
Who would have made me a LARK
to fit my flight pattern, but

he was already married to a girl
named Louise, or Lucy, or Anne with an E,
and I had made a word of my initials
and they all spelled LARD.
                              The point
back then, was to become rich.
And that is what we were, of course,
in the middle of the Great Depression
between those two World Wars, corn
at 2¢ a bushel, clean and shelled.

FIRST THE O

The O fell off my typewriter.
I should have marked the word
when it disappeared. Perhaps
there was a message being sent
in this peculiar way. I felt
I must not interpret otherwise.

The E fell off my typewriter.
The hair stood up on the back
of my neck until I remembered
two letters had interlocked,
perhaps these two had taken
each other off. I relaxed
and had the machine repaired.

The N fell off my typewriter.
I watched the N begin to go,
saw it hunt for a higher line,
then dribble away until no print
was possible, then it was gone,
its small neck broken. Down
the back of mine went chill
after chill. Did someone speak?

Put together in OUIJA style,
what surfacing word was this:
ONE or EON and where were we,
what prophecy was foretold?

Late last night, the O fell
out of my head. I opened
my mouth to cry, no sound
came out. Next the E fell
out of my eye. The E was
there and suddenly was gone.
Then the N fell as if from
a line of clothes, fell in
the grass. I searched
everywhere. Then I knew:
the alphabet was deserting me.
    Where would I go
    for love
    when my words
    were gone.
The L fell out of my head.

THE SUICIDES

The note said: *He'll kill
me. I wrecked his Jaguar XKE.*
The body floated in his father's
bathtub, bloated with pills.

*

Her body hung from the doorsill
on a silk scarf, the same
that framed her face in the open
casket at her request, her requested
wake.

*

One gunshot shattered the birdsong
of the quiet afternoon before the
bird began to sing again in fright.

*

Damn, damn, damn, it isn't that we
don't think of it. I stood
on the bridge looking down
at the water swirls, (he waved
goodbye to passing drivers
as he dove) but there's no way
back up that drop, no way at all.
Water closes over your head
or as in his case, head smashes
ice. And all those rumors

are true, no way now to refute them.
Joy and glee huggermugger in
one dazzled light stroke. Nothing
of our so-called soul remains,
just the last whiplash washing
the spirals against the bridge spokes.
One last message on the telephone
tape: *Call me.*

SHE TOLD ME

                        to remember
the power was in my hands.
I must not waste the worry
beads by letting the craven
under my skin, over my telephone,
into my letter bin. Your revision
is for yourself, she said, nobody
should be allowed to shrink
your heartbeats to mere water
drops from the all-night faucet.
Don't return the calls, she said,
you will spring energy in the wrong
direction, once they have your voice
in their ears, they will want more
and more.
                        But
every "no" I have ever said comes
back like a boomerang loaded with
stones.
                        When I have tried to call
my life my own, I have been left
sitting on the back stoop by myself
gazing into the cellar door, unable
to go up or down.
                        And when I try
not to answer the telephone, I
am wracked with strange lists of
all the impossible people who
might need to talk with me, my
Sears Roebook editor, my out-go
tax lawyer, my younger-than-I-am
mother.

Or all my daughters have
inherited my enormous need to
talk with someone who matters,
and I have turned that terrible
dead ear.

THE GNARLED EGG OF SLEEP

After my neighbor's burglar alarm
cracked open my sleep, I listened
beyond the refrigerator's dropping of
ice eggs for a stir of screen, a ply
of window, a low owl gibbous whirr,
though only the pencil sketch of *West Baffin
Snowy Owls with Egg* came into view
and a covey of grandmothers floated
over my desk top, their eggs already
challenged and perfected, needing
to be blessed.

REINCARNATION

I shouldn't have done it to her.
I should have said, no thank you,
and pushed the gun away. Or
I should have told her that I couldn't miss.
I hadn't shot a gun for twenty years
but I couldn't miss. I meant to try
on purpose, but when the time came
I raised the barrel and sighted down it,
smiled, and six orange juice cans went down
one right after the other.
Annie Oakley, they said, Annie!
Should I have told them who I was?
I'd like to be friends, but she just sits there
the way she sat when I handed back her gun.
I tried to miss, but the smile comes over me.
I tried not to play my brother's saxophone but
the smile comes over me.

HIGH TOR

Above the Boston skyline floats
what singular fowl or bird? From my
eighth floor balcony, my binoculars
waver until they catch the distant curve
of red and yellow striped balloon drifting
across a backdrop Matisse could have painted,
no cloud in sight, just one infinitesimal
inverted tear-drop hangs against azure silk,
no fingers from Michelangelo arms to
hold it up, no Tibetan shirpa making
camp, no Ringling Brothers Barnum and
Bailey tent pole, not even a Cape Canaveral
launch rack   nothing
nothing holds it up. One brush stroke
could paint it out.
                    At the small end
of my field glasses, I shrink to balloon
basket size. Highest on my life list:
balloon travel, silent flight, now crossed
off with a rush of terror only reality
could recognize. I lower my binoculars,
my aim, take the elevator down eight
floors and sit upon the ground.

SMALL BOAT RACE
AT KOLLEGEWIDGWOK

Once for a chamber-pot prize
I crewed for a mother of winners
who taught them all to sail.
(Father, a mass of dignity
succumbing to paralysis
the devil couldn't have dreamed
as a special for hell.)
She whispered, scarce moving her lips
"Breathe gently, don't speak,
don't move at all
and this small wisp of wind
will waft us by those luffing boats."
We sat as silent as possible
sitting in human skin
with all that mechanism going inside
and that small breeze, breath-big,
slid into our sail
and we did glide to an inching victory.
Filled with pride
we accepted the rose-encrusted cup.

We are all moving
toward total paralysis,
but using it as you choose,
simulated, to win,
is like turning the death wish
into a usable tool.

TO CONTEND, TO MATCH UP WITH, TO MUZZLE

I choked on a word at a microphone
somewhere in West Virginia, heard
myself seconds after the fact, wasn't
sure which word I'd stuttered on.
Kept right on reading. Only after
I heard a recording did I learn
with sinking dismay, the word was
cope. The key word. I kept on
going and the point of all
those words went swirling down the well
of my throat, a gutteral clucking sound.
I could have corrected if I'd heard
myself in time. Where was my mind?
I'm afraid it was sailing through
air, back, far back to the place the line
began. To the father who said to his dying
daughter, *You have to cope.* I, overhearing,
thought he had meant to say hope, the only
lifeboat some of us have after we lose laughter
down some fishing hole or other. Now here
I see in my fat dictionary how one of the many
meanings of *cope* is to muzzle by sewing up
the mouth.

THE SHUNTED PARACHUTE

There are some answers I don't
know the questions to. If
the conversation heads toward
those cliffs, I buckle my parachute
tight and try to veer toward
a shallow trail, hoping I will
never have to make that particular
       jump.

> *Don't tell me*
> *how he broke your bones.*
> *Don't tell me when*
> *the fog settled over*
> *your eyes, when*
> *you found the rat*
> *chewing on your heart.*

"In England," he said, "one never asks
'what do you do?'" Tantamount to asking
how rich are you? Or what is your people
class? You *know*. Without asking, you
know the strata. You go on for years
without knowing how your friends
make their livelihood.

In the U.S. of A., we dive in where angels
are using their parachutes. What's your
line? Even before you buckle the seat
belt for Cross Country Flight Number
7QW. "What are you in?" we ask, not
meaning blue suit, or blue funk or which
congregation. We mean: what do you do
for a living? (Lie, hunt germ cases . . . .)

Before I learned the rule, having not
lived that long in England, "What do you
do?" said I. He shifted daintily from
one buttock to the other while his wife
held her startled breath, and answered
"Teach." "And what," I continued
"do you … ?" My reporter's mind
went on feeding queries to my open mouth,
wind rushing by my ears. I ignored
the sound. That parachute never opened.

Fortunately I landed in the foliage of
a huge family tree growing in our veins.
I was badly scratched. See that question-
mark scar on the back of my left hand?
In England I will try to remember to
wear my gloves.

WINTER PASSAGE OUT OF
CHARLOTTE AMALIE

No ticket left.
No passage to be bought
until the seaon after next.
If you thought
of winging back to islands
of the powdered sand,
get out the photographs!
That's as close as you can get
       this year.
Our captain's spirited away.
Full drunk, he toppled from the dock
       one night.
(His feet must have been astonished
that he couldn't float.)

No one to sail his ship.
His ship won't sail with a stone
cold sober captain, and she's too big
for drunks to dare her
       even reefed.

They advertised for a cook
the day we boarded her.
It was us they meant to feed,
and oh we ate our fill, sailing
those haunted waters, while the captain stole
our pirate books and ate his fill
of bawdy cutthroats, drunk and stunning
       and the ship
sailed under your hand or mine,
       reeking of rum.

REMEMBERING METEORA

for Roland Flint

> *And he said: You and I are*
> *intuitive writers, meaning we*
> *have a perceptual dysfunction.*

In Meteora, in the highlands of Greece
on the high pinnacles of the rivers, swept away,
I rode by rope to the mountain-top monasteries,
with their chapel domes, jeweled ceilings
glittering in the half-light, but as my eyes
grew accustomed to the scenes, I saw
they were all of death, death
set in jewels that shone in raucous
color, showing martyrs all, and I hung back,
reckoning with a god who let it happen,
the God who invented intuition.

DOUBLE EXPOSURE BY ANSCO

See the line that frazzles the water?
That's where the river
ice begins. There
in the foreground
is the waterfall.
Only the middle two plunges
are running,
but they look the same
in the photograph
as the two that are frozen stiff.

I have a difficult time
conceiving the freezing
of anything moving
as fast as
water falling.
I have always thought I could not freeze
because I am moving so fast. Now I see
I can be held no matter how quickly I move
by whatever I am exposed to long enough.

Wait, is this an icicle
hanging from my hair?

AT LUNCH YOU TALKED ABOUT
A SHOESHINE IN CHICAGO

but you sent me back to Turkey, and the town
was Canakkale, or was it Kusadasi, no, Canakkale
with my first sight of a Turkish street,
of Turkish women wrapped to their eyes, and on
the streets (I was high on a bus on the way
to Troy) were all those small "cathedrals" carried
by straps on the shoulders of their priests,
their bishops, their cardinals, and I do not
mean to be irreligious, for the gold-encrusted
jewel-bedecked, rainbow-glassed "cathedrals"
were in fact where one set one's foot for
a godly shine — I was high in a bus on the way
to Troy — and I had never had a shoeshine,
never wanted one before, but now I wanted one
desperately as if the good life depended on it,
to set my foot on the straight and narrow
foothold on the golden edifice, the gold-laced
decoration shining in the sun, looking
like pure gold, and the moment was pure
and golden, and I was on a pilgrimage,
a pilgrim's way, in a street in ancient Turkey,
in ancient Canakkale, on my way to the mythical
nine cities walled one upon, around the other,
to magic Troy whose nine lives had died
and been resurrected and I was going there
and I needed my shoes, o my feet, my hooves
polished, and I looked down at my bare feet
in their broken thongs — high in a horse on my way
                    to Troy.

FOOD

Word hangs like eyes peering
between two ears. No chance to

grow up to be anybody. Two O's
and a couple of consonants

couldn't possibly be something
we can't live without. Still

that's what hangs there, the start
of foolish with Orphan Annie eyes.

Tastes like your foot's asleep,
he said, talking of fake chocolate,

And Annie Dillard dared to say
the preying mantis ate the hummingbird,

it was food. Anything is food if
you eat it, isn't it? In last night's

dream I hustled my friends away from
the party after I learned the hostess

planned to eat us. Hostess cupcakes.
Did I go to bed hungry? Don't I always?

IMPULSIVE STROKES

Portrait of Dr Felix Rey — van Gogh 1889

You didn't like the portrait Vincent
painted of you. Whether it looked like
you was not the point. Oddly enough
it looks like my childhood chum Roger
(we called him Tubby) Shanks, without
the beard and mustache, of course, except
he did wear both once in a play I wrote
while you were still alive I see by
the dates of your life/death. Rather,
this picture from the Pushkin Museum
looks the way Tubby might have looked
if he had lived long enough. I learned
long after the fact, he died of chicken
pox. It seemed so unlikely, there being
so much of him to suffer slings and arrows.

Maybe the purple coat with rose buttons
makes you seem so paunchy, Dr Rey, young
Intern of Arles. The buttons don't
button, but it's the shape of your face
that looks like my old friend, the intent
look of your eyes, your cupid mouth. Was
that the part you didn't like? Too much
a woman's mouth, too red for males?
"The nervous background," says the catalogue,
"serves to bring to life the essence of
the sitter's character." Is it a gaily
mottled wallpaper of chicken tracks and
feathers? or impulsive strokes that pick
up your pink ear? Whatever, you considered

it the "effort of a miserable madman" and used it for many years to cover the hole in your chicken house. Today van Gogh's portrait of your colleague, Dr Gachet, also with a background of impulsive strokes brought the impulsive price at Christie's of $82.5 million, a new record.

WALLACE IN LILLIPUT

"If you leave out his personal life,
he was a happy man."

Tied down by all the laws of
middle-class morality,
the guilty paws of Pygmalion,
he climbed the stairs
of his obfuscated words,
his handrail imagination.

Now I know why, when I think
of Stevens walking his Hartford
street, he always turns into
Magritte with key and bowler.
He drew the lines for us
as geographers gave us
latitude, equator,
& astronomers patterned
Ursa Major overhead.

I know now why one
biographer thought
his empathy right for
the writing, where "the poem
is the substitute for the woman
one loves or ought to love."

STARTING

I kept thinking if I waited
until the sun warmed the car
maybe I could start it, since
they said the trouble could
be a frozen gas line. The sun
has come up and gone down and
I have had to call a tow truck
to take the car to the shop again.

I kept thinking if I waited
until the sun warmed my back
maybe the poems would come on,
since they seem to be stuck
somewhere between my fingers
and the typewriter keys. The sun
has come up and gone down
and I have dialed my muse over
and over again and nobody answers,

and when I called that well-known poet
for advice, he said: Some of us
just take to bonzai trees.

THE FEMINIST MISTAKE

If I gathered all the words, you
would not recognize yourself. What
kind of angry stairs run down, what
richness of sliding poles, how many
blades of grass sucked on through
the meadow where a new flower
turns up as often as dawn, as often
as a word to love. I have been
mother to your sonly way, filling
you into that empty mold I have
finally forgiven myself for. But
you wouldn't stay in that quietness,
too much fire and flare, so

I wheeled you through all those
other roles of male-to-me: teacher,
father-confessor, brother-in-wine, in
melody, the old guitar strummer holding
my head over the side of the boat,
the serious planner with the map
marked well in front of us
under the one lamp in the dark room,
the one last try, by heart, you are saying,
learn it by heart, the road out of
the dark, and I know you know the way,
and then I realize I have framed a space
for you too often where I forget
and forget again the name of your
new love.

THE DOWAGER QUEEN

How many stepping stones
of women have you used
to reach this place?
What man have I caressed
who felt like you?
The moment when I knew
I mustn't touch you
came and went so quickly,
I was only briefly unattached
from what we said.
I was resigned
to just recalling
this sweet ache.
I had thought I might
fall in love again
only with institutions.
I have yearned for
my lost love for years.
You have slid quietly
into his place
and I recognized
your skin.
I knew
what your lips would
taste like
before all that kissing.
The wonder of it.
The princess
from the tower
said: Take care of him,

before she went back
to her castle.
And I,
thinking I was playing
the dowager queen,
turned and took
you into my arms,
and to send you away
was wrong.

MUSIC TO WORDS,
WORDS TO MUSIC

I thought I was hunting
a composer to set my words
to music. That night I
discovered I was hunting
a composer to set
to music. He was young
and said he could tell
I was a dancer by the way
I walked. I covered the living
room in a few short bounds
separated by a delicate whirl
that flung my pleated skirt
into a carousel, with all
the figured horses dancing.
O it was a delicious night
with the soft hum of the air
conditioner. And no one to
stop us. If only he hadn't
promised to telephone.

DRAKE ESTATE: SIR PAPA DRAKE
AS HORATIO ALGER

Nothing to be done now. Drake
Estate has wilted in the weeds.
Vines cover the old Dream
and Sleeping Beauty has decayed,
her skull gone long in the teeth,
her flesh under maggots. Truth
was not part of it. On my finger
is more gold than can be mined
through those inglorious years.
I travel backward on a frame of should,
hold hands, stroke sweaty brows
and break into a sweat that will not wash
away. I ought to know these fairy tales
from Once-upon-a to the-end. When
everything else was falling into fire,
this dream of gold held fast from
gold mines in the West to golden England
and the sunken wealth. Please don't,
I begged, and slunk beneath my father's
playing fool and telling his wild dream
to every boy who came to our front door.

I play the fool. I should know
about dreams. Gold or fame or
power, I should know. I drink
my Scotch, my dreams, my inglorious
years. Know the map that skirts
the gold mines. This fool's gold
glistens long into the night.

FOR A GOAT

The sun has come down
and is nibbling along the fence row
a light snack before
he goes to bed.

I way as well be hung
for a goat as a sheep,
whatever that means.

Work, the doctor said,
nodding her head,
work is the only cure.

Do not let him back
into your life,
twice he has used treachery,
a third time
could be fatal. Why

do I not listen, why
do I open myself again,
why are the buzzards ablaze
on every limb of the tree
where the sun is munching.

LOOK IF YOU LIKE
BUT YOU WILL HAVE TO LEAP

W H Auden

Coming most naturally to this encompassing
piece of news, that the sun will rise
without me presently, I ponder no-ness.

I have been dying since my twenty-seventh year.
Scientists have proved the downhill ratio.

I am not sustained. Deriving from ancient women
who lived to eighty, ninety, a hundred and ten.
But simply. Never with this angst, this double
Scotch, this cigarette. Who will look into this
cauldron and fish out anything at all? Wisdom
I hoped was shining, mica-like, out of all these
wizened words. But what the hell! All they will find
here is a Collier brothers' quorum, quatrain, quagmire,
quantum, yellowing papers praising me (why else should
I have kept them), scientific quotes paralyzing my brain.
I do not want to die. That's the whole thing in a nutshell.
I figured when I came to the summit at the racy old age
of fifty, I had ten more good years to write and remiss.
I am not content to cash out at sixty. I am not happy
with withering away. At my age, going for broke,
why should I be crucified? I have carried my winter
across my shoulders like a lambskin, wraithed under
an indelible shelf, why should I be without an endurable
prerogative. *I am capable of becoming myself.*
Move me into an oratory I can answer. Late
reasoning will screw me, wrap my innocent
behind around a tree. We are immutable. I am
merciless. I am trodden. I am drunk.

But the laughter winds. Comes up from
deep cellars where the winds blow rank.
Auden, you devil, you are standing forth
in coats of colors, laughing, holding open the door,
making it all possible, risking *le grand* leap.
　　　Look if you like, but ...

SHE OF THE FLAWED CHARACTER

She knew she was cousin to Freud,
Fraud. She knew how her dreams
governed her life. She hadn't flown
in the cockpit for forty years,
and yet the feel of it was in her
hands, her body bend, only because
she had dreamed again last night
of flying the Martin Marauder
(at night the big fish come in.)
She knew all about the power dreams.
At night she was in control. No one
told her that her actions were wry,
though she knew it. No one said: We
don't do that here. The trouble was
she needed someone to say yes to her
more than once a season.

On the eve of her wedding, she met
the man she thought she should have
married. She carried his image next
to her gizzard for forty years,
married all the while. She tried to
fault the other, but it was her fault.
Of course, it was her Papa all the time.
He was the one she couldn't have. Be
careful what you wish for.

On a New Year's Eve, she threw the pennies
in the yard and wished again. Over the hill
loping along came her Wish saying, Hey!
we've fooled around long enough, now let's
get this thing on the road. Just move
a little further along your life and there

on the corner cleaning his nails with
a matchbook will be the Man You Can't Live
Without. That Wish was full-bearded
by then, a long white tapered beard he
almost tripped over, for his body was
as lively as an elf's. She didn't ask
the right questions. She didn't ask any
questions at all. She just kept moving.
In her head she had figured out that they
would be bad news for each other, *New
York Post*-Headline-Type-Bad-News.
She even began to tell him that. She
said, Tell me whatever you have to say
standing up. He said: You don't want
to see me again? She said: That's right.
He said: But I'm yours. On the route
well marked, Route 66, paved and headed
west, ran all those emotions of a gilded
truck, flags flying, the cheering deafen-
ing. Strike that last scene! milky knees
flashed to her blistered brain. Her stupid
body rejoiced as it hadn't since sex was new
and comic. They fell into each other's
arms. They are still falling. Too late,
pass on, says the guard, pass. They didn't
listen. She got what she wished for. She
still has the same old character flaw.
The man she wished for is the man she
cannot have. His name is Papa. Freud
had nothing to do with it. He only defined
the condition, this yearning that breaks
her apart, the enormous NO that curdles
her joints. What she lives for is
the endless YES.

Ann Darr was born in Bagley, Iowa, graduated from the
State University of Iowa, wrote for NBC and ABC Radio
in New York City. As a pilot during WWII, she flew with
the Women's Airforce Service Pilots (WASP) in the US
Army Airforce. She now teaches at The American Univer-
sity in Washington, DC, and at the Writer's Center in
Bethesda, MD. Honors include a Discovery Award from
the Poetry Center in New York City, a National Endow-
ment for the Arts Fellowship, and a Bunting Fellowship
from Radcliffe.

By Ann Darr:
St Ann's Gut Wm Morrow & Co., Inc. (1971)
The Myth of a Woman's Fist Wm Morrow & Co., Inc. (1973)
Cleared for Landing Dryad Press (1978)
Riding with the Fireworks *Alice James Books (1981)*
Do You Take This Woman ... Washington Writers
Publishing House (1986)
High Dark Watershed Tapes (1978)

Other books by SCOP Publications, Inc.:

Stark Naked on a Cold Irish Morning
by Gabriele Glang

Free State: A Harvest of Maryland Poets
edited by Gabriele Glang

The Dolphin's Arc:
Poems of Endangered Sea Creatures
edited by Elisavietta Ritchie

American Classic: Car Poems for Collectors
edited by Mary Swope and Walter Kerr

How to Travel
by Katharine Zadravec

The Cooke Book: A Seasoning of Poets
edited by Michael Glaser

Wintermost
by Robert Bowie

Rye Bread: Women Poets Rising
edited by Stacy Tuthill

Countdown in Bedlam
by Walter S. Kerr

Rasas & Lament of the Sudra
by Desmond O'Brien

Second Rising
edited by Stacy Tuthill

The Ear's Chamber
edited by Stacy Tuthill

A Language of Hands
by Jean Nordhaus

Owl
by Edward Gold